PRAYER FOR AMATEURS

D1136465

Prayer for Amateurs

Jane Holloway

Series Editor: Michael Green

Hodder & Stoughton
LONDON SYDNEY AUCKLAND

Copyright © 2000 Jane Holloway
Illustrations copyright © 2000 by Taffy Davies

First published in Great Britain in 2000

The right of Jane Holloway to be identified as the Author of
the Work has been asserted by her in accordance with
the Copyright, Designs and Patents Act 1988.

10 9 8 7 6 5 4 3 2 1

British Library Cataloguing in Publication Data
A record for this book is available from the British Library

ISBN 0 340 74578 9

Typeset by Avon Dataset Ltd, Bidford-on-Avon, Warks

Printed and bound in Great Britain by
Clays Ltd, St Ives plc

Hodder and Stoughton
A Division of Hodder Headline Ltd
338 Euston Road
London NW1 3BH

With grateful thanks to
my many friends who have taught me how to pray

Contents

From the Editor . . .

'What? Not another book about prayer?'
  'Yes, just that.'
  'But why?'
  'Because we live in an age when spirituality has returned to centre stage.'

Everyone is into spirituality in some shape or form. Sure, they want their material comforts, but they know instinctively that materialism cannot satisfy the hunger of the human heart. We instinctively yearn to relate to something greater than ourselves. And that is where prayer comes in.

Did you realise that prayer is an almost universal activity? Survey after survey shows that practically everyone prays, occasionally or regularly. They may not engage in any form of organised religion, but they pray.

Yet most of them want to know how to pray more effectively. What is prayer all about? Is it worth lighting a candle? Does it make a difference? How can you learn more about it?

These are some of the questions that this book sets

out to answer. Along with its companion volumes, *Bible Reading for Amateurs*, *Churchgoing for Amateurs*, *Evangelism for Amateurs*, *Holy Communion for Amateurs* and *Theology for Amateurs*, it is written for 'amateurs'.

The word 'amateurs' means two things. First, it suggests people who know they are not much good at prayer and need some help. So this book is deliberately written very simply and assumes nothing. Second, it comes from a Latin word that means 'lovers'. This book is written by someone who loves God a lot and wants to help the rest of us to develop this love relationship with God.

Could you do with a little help in this area? Then *Prayer for Amateurs* is for you!

A final word from me about the author, Jane Holloway. We have worked in partnership for fourteen years, and I have had the opportunity of seeing the reality of her prayer life and the gifted way in which she helps others. So I am delighted that she has agreed to write this book. She is well qualified to do so, as she is the Prayer Co-ordinator of the million-strong Evanglical Alliance and is in close touch with the explosion of prayer happening not only in the UK but also worldwide.

Michael Green
Series Editor

1

Introduction – prayer is for amateurs

As you pick up this book, you may not realise it, but you are joining the growing number of people who are beginning to pray. Here in the UK, there are groups of children meeting before going to school and hundreds of teenagers linking weekly via fax and email across the country. There are inter-church groups praying in many towns, villages and cities. In the London Docklands, over ten thousand people regularly gather to pray for London and Britain. Prayer is happening in prisons, in the workplace and in council offices.

This increase in prayer is not restricted to the UK. At a conservative estimate, there are more than ten million prayer groups in the world today. Christians are taking time out of their daily lives to pray on their own, in small groups and at retreat houses. The world-wide prayer movement has been described as being 'out of control', because it is spreading so fast that it is

impossible to keep records, especially in the Third World. For instance, in October 1999, fifty million people all over the world took up the challenge to pray for the band of nations just north and south of the equator – the '10/40' window – which is the part of the world most resistant to Christianity.

Not only is prayer growing but the gospel is spreading faster than it has ever done in our history. Throughout the world, more than a hundred thousand people become Christians every day. Could there be a connection between this and the growth in prayer?

There were no Christians in Korea a hundred years ago. Now a third of the population of South Korea is vibrantly Christian. What could account for such phenomenal growth? Prayer! Most Christians spend an hour a day from 5 a.m. to 6 a.m. and the whole of Friday night in prayer, and thousands go to the country's famous prayer mountain.

Goiania is a city of 1.2 million people in the heart of Brazil. Today 45 per cent of the population are Christians. Visitors report that there are churches and Christians everywhere. And this growth in Christianity all started when a dedicated radio prayer programme was launched in the city, mobilising over 180,000 Christians to pray.

These stories do not, however, tell the whole story. Even more remarkable is the fact that the people who make up these figures are ordinary church members. They are not professionals but amateurs in prayer.

- Amateurs who believe God is powerful and hears and answers prayer.
- Amateurs who know that prayer is not trying to twist God's arm, but is his chosen way of extending his kingdom.
- Amateurs like the couple I met who started praying with other Christians for their neighbours, and now describe it as 'the best thing we have ever done in our lives'.
- Amateurs like the minister's wife who heads up the radio prayer programme in Goiania.

Amateurs are those who love what they do. Prayer is God's weapon for all his people. It is much too important to leave to the professionals. I am an amateur when it comes to prayer! There is much about it I don't understand and I certainly don't find it easy. But I have discovered that prayer is one of the most exciting and life-changing aspects of being a follower of Jesus Christ.

Prayer lies at the heart of Christianity, and yet most Christians would agree with non-religious people who pray that we all have much to learn about it. Do you recall the massive response to the death of Princess Diana? Millions wanted to pray, but had no idea how to go about it.

So in our next chapter we will look at one of the most common questions asked about prayer – what is it?

A prayer for amateurs

God, I feel pretty hopeless at prayer. Please show me its value and teach me to pray. Amen.

2

Prayer – what is it?

Prayer is essentially relationship with God. And it is this relationship which is at the heart of the Christian faith. It is amazing to realise that the God who created the universe wants you and me to be in regular touch with him. Prayer is a conversation between us and God.

All relationships have to be worked at in order to survive. What holds people together is love built on friendship, daily contact, honest talking and shared lives. And it is the same in our relationship with God. He wants us to talk and listen and to allow our lives to touch his. We pray to God just as we talk with each other – it may be aloud or in silence. Just as we communicate with each other with maybe a look, a smile, a hug, a kiss, so we learn to converse with God by using our senses and our bodies.

But if prayer is a conversation with God, and God is Father, Son and Holy Spirit, which part of God are we talking to? And does it matter?

Praying to God as Father

If you find the idea of God wanting us to pray a little difficult to grasp, you are not alone. Jesus' disciples took a while to get the idea. As Jews they were used to praying, but as they watched Jesus they realised they were missing something. So they asked him to teach them to pray. Jesus told them that they could come to God in prayer as if he was their father (Matthew 6:9). They were amazed! He said they were to use the word *Abba*, which in their language means 'Daddy' or 'dear father'. It was the word that was commonly used by younger children speaking to their fathers.

Prayer is not something we 'say' to a distant God; when we pray, we come as God's child to our Father in heaven. A friend, John, tells the story about one of his grandsons. When Andrew was six years old he spent a week in the summer staying with his other grandparents on their farm. They loved having him and told him many times just how invaluable he was in helping them. When Andrew went home, he enjoyed telling everyone that his grandparents were having trouble running the farm without him. As John was laughing over this, God nudged him. 'John, you've been like little Andrew with me! You've treated me like a helper in the sky.' John was then reminded that the image of Andrew going off on the tractor and sitting on his grandfather's lap was a picture of prayer.

The moments of greatest delight in God's relationship with us are when we, in childlike dependence and faith, climb on to his lap in prayer, put our hand on his hand and pour out our hearts to him.

I met up with a small group from church last night to pray for our minister, who is going to teach in Nigeria for two weeks. It was very evident that we were praying to our heavenly Father who knew everything about the trip. We all left with a profound sense of peace that he would take care of it all.

Praying through Jesus

We pray to our heavenly Father through Jesus, 'for through him we both have access to the Father by one Spirit' (Ephesians 2:18). Jesus taught the disciples that they should ask of the Father in his name (John 14:13–14; 15:16). To pray in his name does not simply mean we use his name as a 'password' or a formula, but rather that when we do so we confess his name and acknowledge that he is the only way to the Father.

As we pray, we direct our minds and thoughts in faith towards God and then share with him what is on our hearts. Praying is as simple as making a phone call. Before the days of direct dialling, everyone had to ring up an operator and ask to be put through to the number wanted. Today we can directly dial to almost anywhere in the world through central phone exchanges. Jesus makes it possible for our prayers

always to get through to our Father in heaven. We will never get the engaged or number unobtainable tones. We don't need different numbers for enquiries, faults or complaints. All our prayers go to the same person at the same place, 'Our Father in heaven' when we pray in the name of Jesus.

Praying with the Holy Spirit

We pray to God the Father, through Jesus and with the help of the Holy Spirit. God knows us through and through. He knew that we would never be able to have the strength to love him 'with all our heart, and mind, and soul' without help. So Jesus left his Holy Spirit to help us. This unseen Spirit of Jesus is our helper, guide and comforter. He is the one who enables us to say Jesus is Lord (1 Corinthians 12:3).

The Holy Spirit is essential for our praying. He prompts us when to pray. He helps us know how to pray, and when we are stuck and don't know what to pray for, he steps in (Romans 8:26ff). He even provides us with a new language (tongues) to pray when ordinary words run out (1 Corinthians 14). Paul Yonggi Cho, the Korean pastor of the largest church in the world, has often spoken of his reliance on the Holy Spirit, whom he calls his 'Senior Partner', and whom he consults before praying and making any sort of decision.

Prayer is a key

Prayer is also a key to understanding God's heart. Richard Foster, the popular American author, movingly describes how God is longing to welcome us 'home'.

> He invites us into the living room of his heart where we can put on old slippers and share freely. He invites us into the kitchen of his friendship where chatter and batter mix in good fun. He invites us into the dining room of his strength, where we can feast to our heart's delight. He invites us into the study of his wisdom where we can learn . . . and ask all the questions we want. He invites us into the workshop of his creativity . . . He invites us into the bedroom of rest where new peace is found, and where we can be naked and vulnerable and free.[1]

And the key to this home – which is the heart of God – is prayer. Prayer not only enables us to talk to God about the things that concern us, but it also helps us to understand God better. The more we discover about who God is and what he longs to see happen in his world, the better we are able to pray, as we shall explore in the following chapters.

- Prayer is not something we have dreamed up – we

are created to be in touch with God. God invented prayer.

- Prayer is not simply saying the same words or prayers at a set time – though regular times of prayer with written prayers is one of the many ways we can pray.
- Prayer is not about trying to change God's mind. It is actually about us coming into line with his mind!
- Prayer is not a matter of reeling off a list of requests – though asking does form a very important part of prayer (see Chapter 7).

But the practice of prayer does raise an important question – why do we need to bother if God knows everything anyway?

A prayer for amateurs

Father God, there is much about you I don't understand. Please help me to get to know you better. Amen.

3

Prayer – why bother?

Does prayer have a place in our fast-paced society at the start of the twenty-first century? It would seem so. More than 65 per cent of people in Britain claim to pray at various points in their lives. That is almost ten times the number you will find in church. This points to a very deep instinct in all human beings, whether they would consider themselves 'religious' or not. For instance, comedian Jack Dee told an interview with the *Daily Mail*, 'I pray on a daily basis but I haven't found any church or religion I can live with.' The demand for retreats has doubled in the last five years, according to the author of *The Good Retreat Guide*. 'People have the house, the relationship, the job – but they say, "Hey, is there another dimension to where my life is going?" ' The need to cry out to a power beyond ourselves is deeply rooted in human hearts.

But does prayer 'work'? This question has fascinated researchers over the years. And each time an experiment is done, it shows that people who believe in God or in prayer generally fare better than those who don't. A recent study (reported in October

1999) found this to be true for heart patients. The researchers studied 990 patients admitted during a year to the Mid-America Heart Institute's coronary care unit. The patients were randomly divided into two groups. In the first group, patients were prayed for daily for four weeks; the second group didn't have anyone assigned to pray for them. After four weeks, the prayed-for patients had suffered about 10 per cent fewer complications, ranging from chest pain to cardiac arrest. 'It's potentially a natural explanation we don't understand yet – a "super- or other-than-natural" mechanism,' said William Harris, who was lead author of the study.

We pray because . . .

But why do we need to pray if God knows everything anyway? We pray because God wants us to come to know him better. We come back to the fact that prayer is all about relationship with a God of love who wants us to be in touch with him. We are not meant to live our lives independently from God. He invites us to draw near and listen to him (Isaiah 55:6). Through prayer we discover more fully who we are. I found it interesting that Cher, when interviewed during her 1999 All-America tour, told how she prayed before each show. Minutes before going on stage each night, she would call the crew together and pray as they all held hands.

We pray because God himself modelled in Jesus a life of prayer. Jesus did not say '*if* you pray', but '*when* you pray'. He did not squeeze prayer into his life and ministry. He slotted in his friendships, ministry and travelling between times of prayer. Jesus needed to have time with his heavenly Father, in order to keep in touch and to know what he should be doing. If he did, so do we. If he needed to have time apart from the rat race, we need to do the same. Jesus was able to be so in tune with his Father because he made time for prayer.

We pray because our prayers matter to God. We may think that our prayer is too small to be noticed. I take great comfort from the fact that God thinks his people praying to him is so important that he halts the worship in heaven. We read in the book of Revelation that for half an hour the worship was stopped so that the prayers of the saints (which is us!) could be heard, received and then sent back down to earth to make a difference (Revelation 8:1–5). God hears the prayers of every person.

I remember being in a group that was exploring whether the Christian faith was relevant. Some felt it was real and others not. One man prayed at the end of the meeting: 'God, I don't know if you exist, but if you do please show yourself to me.' Within a few weeks he came back and shared how he had encountered Jesus. God had heard the cry of his heart, and today he is now leading his own church.

We pray because God wants to extend his kingly rule in his world and he has chosen us to work with him. In this partnership of friendship, God can do things through us that he could not do if we did not pray. He has chosen prayer to be a mighty weapon by which we can draw on his power and strength (see Chapter 10).

He wants to bring change first in ourselves. The more we find ourselves caught up in conversations with God and invite him to be part of our daily lives, the more we will find our moods, our thoughts and our priorities are changed (Colossians 3:10). As Basil Hulme said, 'If people pray their consciousness becomes more selective. It is very difficult to be a praying person and then to go out and be beastly to our neighbour.'

He wants to bring change to others. He is longing for us to be channels of his love, his peace and his healing and to enable all people to come to know his Son Jesus Christ. I heard about a small church, which found itself in the position of having only seventy-three members, all of whom would be classed as 'older people'. They knew the church would have to close unless something happened, so they decided to 'try prayer'. They started to pray that ten new members would join in the next year. Within four months, seven new people had joined the church. By the end of the first year, thirteen more had joined, including some young families. That story bears out Archbishop William Temple when he said, 'People tell me that answers to prayer are merely coincidences. I can only reply that when I pray coincidences happen and when I stop praying they stop happening.'

We pray because we have nowhere else to turn. As this Bulgarian pastor, who was imprisoned for his faith, says: 'Under such circumstances, the only thing no one can do is take away the opportunity to pray. I realised that when I needed prayer most, God deprived me of the chance to do anything else. In my loneliness I could be in constant fellowship with God – the only source of power in my life . . . In prison I came to know that God can satisfy our needs in two different ways – by giving us what we pray for and by delivering us from the need for which we pray . . . I was hungry for most of the time. Then I prayed, "Lord, you fed five thousand people with five loaves of bread and two fish. Here there is only one of me, so even crumbs will be enough." God did not give me more bread, but he did free me from the feelings of hunger . . . In prison I realised that we have the mightiest weapon given to us by God – prayer.'

So if prayer is so important to God, let's see how we can do it. As there are many elements to prayer we will look first at worship.

A prayer for amateurs

Lord Jesus, I want to thank you for the gift of prayer. Please help me to want to bother to pray. Amen.

4

Prayer is worship

Worship lies at the very heart of what it means to be human. For every man, woman and child is created to worship God and enjoy his company for ever. That is why worship, which means giving God his worthship, is at the centre of the Christian faith.

In the Old Testament there are many songs of worship, especially in the book of Psalms. One of my favourites is Psalm 145 which begins, 'I will exalt you, my God the King; I will praise your name for ever and ever.' David goes on to praise God for who he is and because of what he is like. And we need to do the same in our own words.

Jesus praised God. On one occasion, as the seventy-two disciples returned to report back to Jesus after being sent out on a short-term mission, Jesus burst into a prayer of worship. 'I praise you, Father, Lord of heaven and earth, because you have hidden these things from the wise and learned, and revealed them to little children' (Luke 10:21). And we learn from the book of Revelation that heaven is full of God's people praising and worshipping Jesus the Lamb who is 'worthy... to receive glory and honour and power' (Revelation 4:11).

Worship is not something we do before we pray – worship in itself is prayer. Some of the most dynamic prayer meetings I have attended have been when we have spent most of the time in worship. Jesus wants us to spend time in worship. We read in Luke chapter 10 how Jesus visited the house of two sisters. Martha was busy preparing for Jesus' visit to her house and getting the meal ready, but Mary, we are told, didn't bother to lift a finger to help her sister. She just sat at Jesus' feet. Martha got cross and accused her of wasting time, but Jesus made it clear that Mary had chosen the better thing (Luke 10:38–42).

The Taizé Community in France bears witness to the power of worship. Fifty years ago, a young Swiss man gathered around him a few friends and started a community founded on worship and prayer. Today many thousands of people visit each year and are profoundly blessed and renewed by living in an atmosphere of worship.

Each of us will worship in contrasting ways, because we all relate to God differently. What seems perfectly right for me may seem strange to you! Although we are clearly told by God not to make idols of him in any way, many Christians find using symbols an aid to worship. It may be a lighted candle to focus on Jesus 'the light of the world', or a vase of flowers or a single bloom to remind us to worship the creator God. It may be a cross – hung on a wall or held in the hand – that helps us to meditate on what Jesus did for us. Some Christian traditions use icons – pictures that frame our thoughts and prayers. Others use prayer-beads, or burn incense.

It is also good to use words, whether spoken or sung. Finding words to praise God should not be difficult, for when you are talking with someone you love, you don't worry so much about what you say, you just say it. In fact, if you are talking to a baby, you probably won't even use proper words! When we care deeply about a person, we will want to speak of our love and appreciation.

When we do find it hard to praise God (and we all find it hard sometimes!), we should ask God to show us why. It might have to do with our stubbornness and pride, when we just won't admit that we can't manage on our own. Or it could be because we are going through a crisis, illness or bereavement. Praising God has nothing to do with how we feel at any given time, but everything to do with who God is and the fact that he deserves our praise at all times. As we are reminded in the letter to the Hebrews, we are to bring 'a sacrifice of praise' (Hebrews 13:15). A few years ago I gathered with about two thousand other people at the NEC in Birmingham, to pray for people known to us who have turned their backs on God ('prodigals'), an event organised by the Prayer for Revival team. We spent much of the day in worship to our God, who we knew was more concerned about our loved ones than we could ever

be! He did indeed hear our prayers, as we have since heard of many scores of prodigals who have come back to God again.

How can we worship as we pray?

We can use the names of Jesus. The very familiar second line of the Lord's Prayer can trip off our tongues without our fully realising its meaning. 'Hallowed be your name' means to honour or praise his name. There are many names for God in the Bible – in fact, more than enough for each day of the year. For example Jesus is: almighty, bread, counsellor, deliverer, exalted, friend, great, holy, intercessor, judge, king of kings, Lord, master, name above all names, obedient, prince of peace, ruler, shepherd, teacher, understanding, vine, worthy. Each of these names tells us something about his character. By taking one of these and spending a few moments reflecting on what it means to us, we can praise God.

We can use music, even if we are not particularly musical. *Songs of Praise* on the television continues to attract high ratings as people sit and listen (and often sing along!) to favourite hymns on a Sunday evening. I use a hymn or song book and quietly sing, hum the tune, or just read the words. Sometimes I put on a tape or CD of Christian songs and allow myself to be caught up in praise and wonder. I find this especially useful on long train journeys or in the car sitting in traffic jams.

If we can't find our own words then the Bible is our best resource book, especially the book of Psalms. The writers of these wonderful praise songs so often seem to sum up exactly what I want to say when I can't find the words to say it! I know Christians who always read at least one psalm every day to help them learn more about God and about prayer.

One of the most exciting developments in recent years has been a new desire for Christians to meet together to praise and celebrate our God. Thanks to the March for Jesus organisation, many Christians world-wide have had the opportunity to go out on to the streets to praise and pray for their communities, towns and nations. I shall never forget taking part in the first global march in London, when I gathered with thousands of others in Hyde Park to pray for our nation and its future and for the needs of our world.

As dawn broke on 1 January 2000 Christians all over the world met together to praise and worship through the day. In Cardiff, over sixty thousand packed the new Cardiff stadium to celebrate Jesus' two-thousandth birthday in a *Songs of Praise* that was broadcast to many nations. In Nottingham, three thousand Christians marched into the Market Place, at the invitation of the City Council, for a service of praise and prayer to mark the historic place that the Christian Church has in the life of the city and county.

However we choose to worship, we would do well to cultivate the habit of becoming someone who takes worship seriously. Why not take five minutes today and spend them in God's presence, praising him for his love and faithfulness to you?

We will now look at the next element of prayer: saying sorry, or confession.

A prayer for amateurs

Almighty God, you are so great and wonderful. Teach me how to really worship you today and every day. Amen.

5

Prayer is saying sorry

If the prayer of praise is lifting our hearts to God, then the prayer of saying sorry, or confession, is opening our hearts to God.

Of all the different aspects of prayer, this is probably one of the most difficult. Which of us likes to admit we have done things wrong? You only have to be around children for a short time before something happens that requires an apology. After the tears have stopped, the pride has been conquered and those three special words 'I am sorry' uttered, everyone is happy as play resumes once again. And if we think children find it hard, adults find it more difficult to admit they have been wrong!

Sometimes we can be hesitant to pray, because we know the state of our hearts and our lives. And that reticence is actually very appropriate, for God does know everything about us and all that we do wrong. But all he wants is for us to come to him and confess our sins. Confession is all about acknowledging we have sinned, naming what we have done wrong and bringing it out into the open. When we have done that, God can wipe away the sin and bring healing and reconciliation.

Jesus' moving story of the prodigal son makes this very clear (Luke 15:11–32). We meet the prodigal son first and learn that he has rejected his father's love and has left home, taking his inheritance with him. But the glamour fades and the money runs out. When he comes to his senses, feeding the pigs, he decides to return home and say sorry. His father is still on the look-out, and when he sees him coming, he runs to meet him and welcomes him home to a banquet. The elder son watches and becomes very jealous, so much so that the father has to reprimand him. The prodigal's confession means he is welcomed home. The elder son is left with a difficult decision as to whether he can forgive his younger brother and once again be reconciled to both his father and his brother.

Unconfessed sin stifles prayer. King David realised this truth after his affair with Bathsheba: 'If I had cherished sin in my heart the Lord would not have listened' (Psalm 66:18). Saying sorry helps us to keep in touch with God. 'If we claim to be without sin, we deceive ourselves and the truth is not in us. If we confess our sins, he is faithful and just and will forgive us our sins and purify us from all unrighteousness' (1 John 1:8–9).

The story is told about a famous preacher, Smith Wigglesworth, who refused to pray for a sick woman in one of his meetings. When she asked him why, he told her it was because she had bitterness in her heart towards another woman in the service. She then went up to the woman and gave her a formal handshake. Wigglesworth shouted, 'Woman, you will die of your sickness if you don't repent and make things right!' As five thousand people looked on, she began to sob and ask for forgiveness, and the other woman did the same. Suddenly it started to spread all through the crowd, and people began to forgive one another. Wigglesworth shouted again, 'Come on up and I will pray for you now.' She answered, 'You don't have to. God has just healed me.'

How do we say sorry?

First, we come to God humbly and tell him what we know to be wrong in what we have said, done or thought. Second, we humbly ask for his forgiveness. Jesus told a story of two men who went to the synagogue to pray – a Pharisee (a religious leader) and a tax collector (who would have been looked down on by society). The Pharisee prayed about himself and how proud he was of himself and all that he did for others. The tax collector could only utter the words 'God, have mercy on me, a sinner.' Jesus made it very clear that it was the humble prayer of the tax collector that was heard by God in heaven (Luke 18:10–14).

We do not need to use special prayers: our own words will do. But you may find using prayers from a book or from the Bible helpful, for example Psalm 51. If you are not sure what to say sorry for, try looking back over the previous day. Ask the Holy Spirit to shine his searchlight in your recent life – and confess what he shows up. We will find we need to make time for confession daily, and for most of us many times a day! You may find it useful to use the same prayer. Christians in the Eastern Orthodox Church use 'Lord Jesus Christ, Son of God, have mercy on me, a sinner.' Other favourite prayers are 'Lord, forgive me' or 'Lord, I'm sorry.' Why not choose your own favourite Bible verse or prayer and use it daily?

Saying sorry is, however, only part of the story. Third, we need to ask God to help us stop sinning and to change our attitudes and lifestyle. True confession will lead to our turning round and changing direction – which is called repentance. King David not only said sorry, he also changed his ways. When Jesus called Zacchaeus the tax collector to become one of his followers, his heart was changed. He immediately knew he needed to pay back all the money he had in effect stolen from his customers (Luke 19:8).

Fourth, we need to receive the cleansing that God offers. God in his love has made a way for us to receive forgiveness. We receive it by faith from a God who hears and answers our prayers. It sounds simple – it is simple.

Fifth, we need to forgive others, as the Lord's Prayer reminds us: 'Forgive us our sins as we forgive those who sin against us.' When Peter asked Jesus,

'How many times must I forgive?' Jesus replied, 'Seventy-seven times,' indicating that we need to keep forgiving and forgiving and forgiving. Jesus went on to tell the story of an unforgiving servant, which clearly shows how forgiveness for our own sins is actually dependent on how we extend forgiveness to others (Matthew 18:21–35). As C.S. Lewis put it, 'To be a Christian means to forgive the inexcusable, because God has forgiven the inexcusable in you.'

It is hard to pray for forgiveness, especially if we have been wronged. In 1987 an IRA bomb went off in Northern Ireland on Remembrance Day and buried Gordon Wilson and his twenty-year-old daughter Marie in rubble. Gordon caught the attention of the world when he spoke from his hospital bed after Marie's death: 'I have lost my daughter, but I bear no grudge. Bitter talk is not going to bring Marie back to life. I shall pray, tonight and every night, that God will forgive them.' He spent the rest of his life until he died in 1995 working for peace in Northern Ireland.

Saying sorry is not just confined to the individual. There are times when, as families and communities, we all need to say sorry for wrongs done against God and others. In some churches this takes place regularly in Sunday worship, when time is given to a prayer of confession for corporate sin. This type of confession is very powerful. And in 1983, not long before the Iron Curtain was lifted, Pope John Paul II visited his homeland of Poland. As thousands of people began to gather for a large open-air mass, they were organised to march in groups of parishes. It was reported that as they walked past the Communist Party Headquarters they chanted, 'We forgive you, we forgive you.' They maintained that spirit of forgiveness in spite of all the atrocities that were carried out against the Catholic Church. In time the regime crumbled.

A prayer for amateurs

Loving Father, I know I am not always honest with you or myself. I am sorry. Please forgive me and help me to start again. Amen.

6

Prayer is giving thanks

Thanksgiving should be one of the strongest motivations to pray as we are able to express our gratitude to God for what he has done for us. We worship God for *who he is*, and we give thanks for *what he has done*. This follows on naturally from praise and confession.

Thanksgiving has been a vital part of all worship down the centuries. God ordained that the 'thank-offering' was an integral part of the worship of ancient Israel (cf. Leviticus 7:12). Giving thanks occurs many times in the psalms and also at other times – for example, when the wall at Jerusalem was finished (Nehemiah 12:31). The same note of thanksgiving is carried into the New Testament. Mary gave thanks as she willingly accepted the role of being the mother of Jesus (Luke 1:46–55). Simeon thanked God when he met the baby Jesus and realised that he was indeed the long-awaited Saviour (Luke 2:28–32). Jesus was thankful. Before giving out the five loaves and two fishes to feed the five thousand 'he gave thanks and broke the loaves' (Luke 9:16). Thanksgiving was a hallmark of the early Church. St Paul in his writings is constantly either thanking God for his brothers and sisters – 'I thank my God through Jesus Christ for all of you' (Romans 1:8) – or encouraging his readers to be thankful (Ephesians 5:20).

Is it really possible to be that thankful when life seems to be against us and we are ourselves in the middle of pain and suffering? Paul poses two challenges: give thanks *for* all circumstances (Ephesians 5:20) and 'give thanks *in* all circumstances' (1 Thessalonians 5:18). I think he is encouraging us to give thanks to the God who is over all that we experience and face. We do not thank him for all the adverse or painful circumstances themselves, but place the situations and people into God's hands and in faith trust him for the outcome. We cannot change things – but we can cry out to God who can bring change. And the result? We can then be given the strength to cope with what we have to face and can be prevented from becoming cruel, angry or bitter.

When I meet people who are going through suffering, bereavement or illness, it is usually easy to recognise those who are seeking to trust God in the midst of the pain. I think of a family who moved to Canada so the husband could do a three-year postgraduate study programme. Shortly after they arrived, first his wife and then one of his children was diagnosed with cancer. During the long hard months of treatment that followed the one thing that kept them going as a family was a daily time with

God to draw on his strength and his love.

However, the reality is that many of us do find saying 'thank you' difficult or even impossible. And this affects God. When Jesus tells the story of the healing of the ten lepers, there is a real sense of disappointment at the end (Luke 17:11–19). This was powerfully brought home to me when a group of us acted out this passage in a drama workshop. After prayerfully reading through the text, ten of the group chose to be lepers and I was put in the role of Jesus. The group creatively acted out how they would have been affected by leprosy. As I approached them, they cried out, 'Lord, have mercy on us!' and I in turn said, 'Go and show yourselves to the priest.' I found that my heart sank as they walked off 'healed', and I was so pleased when one did come back. As we talked about it afterwards, it was interesting to find that all nine felt guilty that they had not said 'thank you'. It reminded them of how often they failed to thank God. I also realised that God does mind if we are ungrateful.

How do we give thanks?

We should be thankful for the past and should pause to remember how God has been faithful as we look back on our own lives and those of our families, friends, church and nation. We will find ourselves giving thanks for God's goodness, for giving us Jesus,

'the indescribable gift', for offering us forgiveness and for the gift of the Holy Spirit.

We should be thankful for the present – for today. Most of us in the West take our everyday luxuries of food, home, water, clothes, health and money for granted. It can be helpful to ask the question: 'What am I grateful for today?' And to respond in prayer accordingly.

We should also be thankful for the future. We will not know what the long-term future is, but we do know that Jesus has gone before us and our future is safe in his hands. Rather than worrying about the future, we ought instead to turn our concerns into prayers of thanksgiving. 'Do not be anxious about anything, but in everything, by prayer and petition, with thanksgiving, present your requests to God. And the peace of God, which transcends all understanding, will guard your hearts and your minds in Christ Jesus' (Philippians 4:6–7).

We can encourage the habit of giving thanks by adopting a simple daily routine. For example, we can pause to give thanks as we get up in the morning, make a cup of coffee, turn on and off the computer, work through a pile of ironing or end a phone call. There is a long Christian tradition of taking time at the end of the day to stop and reflect back as well as look ahead. Simply find a quiet place and in your mind look back over the day and recall what you are thankful for; then turn that into praise and prayer.

If you find that your prayer life has become dull,

try spending over half the time you are able to give to God in thanksgiving. I guarantee it will totally change your prayer time and your attitude to life! Oprah Winfrey has told of how, a number of years ago, she started to write down five things every day that she is thankful for; she says that it has transformed her life.

A prayer for amateurs

Our Father in heaven, thank you for loving me, for caring for me, for forgiving me. Help me to become a thankful and grateful person. Amen.

7

Prayer is asking

We come now to the next part of prayer – asking or, as it is sometimes called, supplication. I know that many of us find asking difficult, especially if we are British! Can I really pray for myself – surely that is selfish? We are sometimes reticent about praying for others – might we be interfering? In any, case, do I have the right to pray for someone else – what if I pray the wrong thing?

We need to remember that asking is right at the heart of our relationship with God. He has made it this way. When a child comes up to you with a big smile and asks you to help them, what do you feel? I know I am pleased that they want my help. It is the same with God. He is pleased when we come and ask him. As the nineteenth-century preacher Charles Spurgeon said, 'Asking is the rule of the kingdom.'

We can take encouragement from Jesus. He often asked for help from his heavenly Father when he was on earth. He prayed for himself – before making decisions, before his baptism, before choosing his disciples and before he went to the cross. He also prayed for others. In coming to his Father and asking for his guidance, Jesus was ensuring that he was in line with God's plans for him. If it was important for Jesus, it is important for us.

Jesus told a story about prayer (Luke 11:5–13). A friend opens his home at midnight to a hungry traveller, who has been on a long journey. Out of courtesy, the friend must feed this traveller, but he finds that there is no bread in the house. So he goes to the house of a wealthy friend, knocks hard on the door and wakes him up. The man is not best pleased, but in the end he has no choice but to get up and give his friend the bread. We are like the friend in the middle, who is not able to meet the needs of his hungry traveller but knows someone who can. Jesus ends with a beautiful promise to encourage us in our praying: 'Ask and it will be given to you; seek and you will find; knock and the door will be opened to you' (Luke 11:9–10).

Praying for others

As that story illustrates, God wants us to pray for others. As we pray for them, we put ourselves in the position of standing in the gap between them and God, and then ask God to help them. This form of prayer is sometimes called intercession (a term used in a court of law to mediate and plead for a case). There is no greater privilege than to pray for someone else. This is what Jesus does: 'he always lives to intercede for them' (Hebrews 7:25).

Intercession has been described like this. Someone comes to God with a request that is in line with his will. Jesus, sitting at the right hand of the Father, says, 'Father, do it for him.' Touched by the need, the Father and Jesus send the Holy Spirit to prompt a Christian to stand in the gap in prayer for however long it takes.

What should we pray about?

We should start by asking God and finding out what he wants. So often we rush in with our own shopping lists and we forget to stop and to listen (see Chapter 8). We learn much from the story of Abraham praying for Lot in Genesis 18:16–33. As the story unfolds we see how God starts off the conversation and how Abraham stops and listens. As Abraham understands what is on God's heart, he begins to pray about Lot and the city of Sodom until God moves on. In the next chapter it is interesting to see how God answers Abraham's heartfelt prayers for Lot. Intercessory prayer means we need to listen to God, wait for God, ask from God and then trust God with the outcome.

We can ask by using the same questions that we might ask another person. Who do you want me to pray for? What do you want me to ask for? Why is such and such happening? What are the obstacles which need to be removed for your will to be done? What is your will for them in this situation? Why is nothing apparently happening? What do you want me to do next?

We can always pray about everyday basic needs for ourselves and others, like health, food, clothes, relationships and finance, as we are told to do in the Lord's Prayer – 'give us today our daily bread'. Many have found using the acronym of BLESS a very useful framework for prayer for friends, family and neighbours. When we ask God to bless another person, we are in effect asking for God to give them all of his love, peace, joy and help. Working through each letter means that we cover every aspect of their life.

Body and health needs – pray for all physical needs;
Labour – pray for work, unemployment, finance issues, retirement;
Emotional – pray for joy, peace, relief from stress;
Social – pray for relationships at every level: home, family, friends, work;
Spiritual – for deepening of faith, holiness, need for repentance.

The 5 × 5 prayer challenge using BLESS has transformed many lives. Simply start to pray for one person (neighbour, work colleague, family member) for five minutes a day for five days for five weeks. At the end of that time, share with someone else what you have learned about yourself, God and prayer, and look for how God has answered your prayers!

The Schultz family took up this challenge, and their seven-year-old began to pray for her two friends at school. One day, one of their mothers, Sheila, stopped Jean Schultz on the street and asked if she could come to church on Sunday. She went, and decided that it was time she started to follow Jesus. Then she joined the Schultz family in praying for her husband, Bill. When Bill returned from a long business trip, Joe Schultz called in. Bill then told him how, one morning while he was away, he had found himself praying, and now he wanted to find out about God! In a matter of months, the whole family was baptised and worshipped together in church.

We can pray for 'his will to be done on earth as it is in heaven'. This is where we ask that all of our lives (our use of time, finance, relationships, etc.) are submitted totally to his will. I usually start with a time of saying sorry before moving on to pray for those closest to me. Then, if time permits, I go wider and pray for my church, my workplace, and maybe an item in the news. We need to learn to start in our own backyard and move out, led by the Holy Spirit, just as a pebble dropped into water sends ripples to fill the whole pond.

Who should we pray for?

St Paul, writing to Timothy, said, 'I urge, then, first of all, that requests, prayers, intercession and thanksgiving be made for everyone – for kings and all those in authority, that we may live peaceful and quiet lives in all godliness and holiness. This is good, and pleases God our Saviour, who wants all to be saved and to come to a knowledge of the truth' (1 Timothy 2:1–4). He is basically saying pray for everyone!

But how can we do that? Research in the United States has shown that each person tends to pray for one of four categories, people, issues, events and communities, though it is my experience that we often pray for things in all four areas! Some will major on praying for family, friends, neighbours, work colleagues, missionaries or leaders in our church, communities or nation. For instance, I know of a group of Christians who regularly put on prayer breakfasts for their MPs. Once or twice a year they invite key leaders in the community, including MPs, to meet with praying Christians, so they can hear from them first-hand what pressures they face and learn how to pray for them.

Others may be more concerned with issues such as children, education, abortion, homelessness or poverty. One friend of mine was given a real burden to pray for her local school and the children and staff. She asked a friend to join her, and together they prayed each week for this school. After the holidays her husband (a local minister) was asked to go in and take some assemblies. To their amazement, without any invitation, a number of children approached them wanting to become Christians. There are now a number of children's Alpha groups happening in this school, with the full permission of the staff.

Others will be prompted to pray for their communities – streets, shopping centres and villages. A marked drop in juvenile crime in Arnold, Nottinghamshire, has followed the setting up of a project to foster co-operation between fifteen local churches and the police. The area police commander, who is behind the initiative, attributes this improvement to a combination of prayer and practical action. 'The prayers appear to be receiving answers. People could say it's coincidence – I think it's more God-incidence.'

Other people will focus their prayers on specific events in their workplace, in the life of their church, in their communities or in the media.

And all of us will ask when we need help, whether for ourselves or for others. I vividly remember when I had to pray for a burglar to be caught. The flat where I was living in central Oxford had been robbed two days running, in spite of the fact that we had changed the locks. As the police were getting worried, they decided to leave a policeman in the hallway on duty all night. I then resolved, together with the friends who lived in the downstairs flat, that we would pray

this burglar back into the house. We told the police-man and started to pray, with my other flatmate acting as watchman upstairs. As we prayed, the man approached the back door, which we had left open. I shall never forget the policeman greeting him with the standard phrase: 'Good evening, sir, you are under arrest!' After a fight in the hall, he was taken away and we were safe again.

During the Welsh revival at the beginning of the twentieth century, one of the leaders of this extraordinary move of God, Evan Roberts, was asked what was the secret. 'There is no secret! Ask and you shall receive.' The challenge for us is to do just that.

A prayer for amateurs

Loving Lord, please forgive me when I am slow to ask. Help me to be bold, persistent and wise so that your name may be glorified. Amen.

8

Prayer is listening

Much of what we have looked at about prayer has centred on our talking to God – giving him praise and thanks, asking for his forgiveness and for specific prayers for ourselves and others. We can easily make the mistake of thinking that prayer is just talking to God. But it takes two to have a real conversation. We need to learn how to listen to God and receive from God, and so learn how best to pray for ourselves and for others. Prayer is not a monologue but a dialogue.

So how does God speak?

He *speaks*, primarily through the Bible, a book written down many centuries ago and inspired by his Holy Spirit. This is not, of course, an audible voice. But we can have a real sense, when certain passages of scripture are read, that God is saying something as old truths are brought home in new ways or we are again made aware of just how much

God loves us. Once, when starting a new job that was daunting, I was reading the story of David going to fight Goliath (1 Samuel 17:39ff). When I came to the part where David determines to go trusting in God and not in the armour that Saul has lent him, I realised that this applied to me in my situation. I often try to listen to the Bible like that and let it speak to me.

God may *speak* through other people. It may be a stranger or someone you know well, who in the middle of a conversation will speak words that help, guide, comfort or challenge. God may *speak* through dreams or visions. Today in parts of the world where it is not possible to talk openly about the Christian faith, many hundreds are turning to follow Jesus. When asked why, many reply that they have seen Jesus in a dream. God may *speak* through the beauty of creation, a gut feeling, a nudge, a sense of something not being right in an event or a conversation. He may *speak* through books, the media and through day-to-day circumstances.

Jesus spoke very clearly about the need to recognise his voice above all the other noise that is around us (John 10:27). But how do we learn to listen?

By meditating on the Bible

Meditation on God's Word is like chewing food which, when digested, becomes part of us. We learn to meditate when we read scripture while asking the Holy Spirit to speak to our inner souls. First, we need to slow down and open our minds and hearts to God. Second, we must ask him to lead us by his Holy Spirit as we read and re-read a short passage of scripture. We should stop and reflect, especially if a word, a phrase or an idea becomes a particular focus. We should then respond in prayer as God leads – which might be for ourselves or for others. If it is a verse of scripture it is good practice to memorise it or make a note of it for future reference.

By making friends with silence

A great French saint of the nineteenth century, the Curé d'Ars, noticed an old farm worker who used to come into his church and just sit there. One day he asked him what he was doing while he sat in church, and the reply was, 'I look at him, and he looks at me, and we understand one another.'

That story shows us another side of prayer, that of contemplative prayer, which is not so much about words and activism, but about being silent in the presence of God. It is for anyone who wishes to enter into a deeper understanding of God and his love for them and for his world. You begin by finding a place to sit (or lie down) and relax in order to become aware of God's presence. As you open yourself to him, reach out to him in love and surrender all your concerns and feelings to him. As you hand over your sins and receive his forgiveness, you remain in an attitude of listening silence. You may praise. You may pray for others. You may just rest in him. It will take a while to get into the discipline of being able to stop, relax, tune in to God and to listen. Whether you pray with others or on your own, allow silence to invade your personal space as you listen to the God who is in you and around you (Psalm 62:5).

By prayer-walking

Prayer-walking is praying 'on site with insight', as described by Graham Kendrick, a modern hymn-writer and one of the founders of March for Jesus. Prayer-walking is simply asking God to help us to see, hear and feel things we do not normally pick up when we rush from place to place. We can prayer-walk on our own or with others. It is not difficult and can be done by anyone, anywhere, at any time. Before you start, ask the Holy Spirit to cleanse and guide you. Walk along with your eyes open, listening to God and using what you see to prompt your prayers. For example, if you see children, you may feel prompted to pray for them and their protection. As you return, make a note to share with others in your church what you have felt. It is also possible to 'prayer-walk' if you are not able to go out. Use your imagination, walk down your road and lift to God in prayer needs which come to mind.

Prayer-walking is a very powerful form of prayer. One of the most remarkable answers to prayer came from a group which was prayer-walking in Gloucester. As they came to a certain road, they felt a great sense of pain and sorrow. They were led to ask the Lord to reveal whatever was hidden in that place. It later turned out to be the site of many murders, as the Wests were brought to justice.

As we learn to listen to God, so we learn to pray as he prompts. We may find ourselves praying for an individual. An American missionary who worked in a field hospital in Africa was sharing a story with his church when he was home on leave. He told how, every fortnight, he had to make a two-day bicycle journey through the jungle to a town to buy medicines and supplies. This meant spending one night in the jungle. One day when he came to the town he saw two men fighting. As one of them was injured, he treated him before buying the supplies. Two weeks later he returned to the town. The young man he had treated approached him and told of how he and some friends had followed him into the jungle on his last visit. 'We were about to kill you when we saw you were surrounded by twenty-six armed guards. All of my five friends saw them. We were afraid and left you alone.' At this point in his talk, the missionary was interrupted by a member of the congregation, who asked when this incident occurred. When told the date, the man took over the story. 'On the night of the incident in Africa it was morning here, and I was preparing to go and play golf. I was about to putt when I felt a strong urge to pray for you. In fact I couldn't continue the game, and I called some men in the church to meet me in the sanctuary to pray for you.' He then asked the men who had met to pray with him to stand. The missionary was not concerned with who they were – he was too busy counting how many he saw. There were twenty-six.

We may be directed to pray for our community. The minister of a large church in Notting Hill in London was challenged by the violence that erupted at the Notting Hill Carnival in the 1980s. He has since told of how he felt 'convicted' by God to pray for the violence to cease. He took this seriously and called the whole church to pray. Within a couple of years the violence had stopped. In last year's carnival, there were only seven arrests, even though two million people joined in this great celebration.

And all these stories would not have happened had the amateurs in prayer not been listening!

A prayer for amateurs

Lord Jesus, how I long to be able to hear your voice today.
Please still my heart and mind and help me to listen. Amen.

9

Prayer is joining with others

It would be very easy to think that prayer is just something we do on our own, especially as we live in such an individualistic culture. But nothing could be further from the truth. There is no such thing as 'solitary' prayer. As we pray, we join with God and Jesus Christ linked by the Holy Spirit, who helps us to cry 'Abba, Father' (Romans 8:15–16). Even if we are physically on our own, we are never alone.

If we look at the Lord's Prayer we find it is a corporate prayer. It starts by saying '*Our* Father', not 'my Father', and continues with 'give *us our* daily bread', 'forgive *us our* sins' and 'lead *us* not into temptation'. Jesus also taught about the importance of agreement and unity in prayer when 'two or three come together in my name' (Matthew 18:19–20). The early Church put his teaching into practice and the disciples made prayer together a priority (Acts 2:42ff). As they sought the Lord and the power of his Holy

Spirit the Church grew and spread through the world.

Praying with others is one of the most exciting and encouraging ways to pray. And there are so many ways to do it!

We can pray together in a church service or event

While each denomination has different ways of worship, most do include a time of corporate prayer. This is usually, though not always, led from the front. You may be one of those who find it difficult to concentrate and find yourself thinking of lists of jobs to be done or the Sunday lunch! But try to concentrate your thoughts on the words that the leaders are using (some people repeat them silently so as to make them their own) or picture in your mind an image of the person or situation being prayed for.

One of the responses we are often asked to make is to say 'Amen', either at the end of a specific prayer or at the end of a time of prayer. Amen means 'I agree' or 'so be it'. It is powerful because it shows that we are all in agreement with the prayer that has been prayed.

We can pray in a Prayer Triplet

One of the most popular ways of praying together in Britain over the last fifteen years has been in groups of three, or Prayer Triplets. These were first started in preparation for Billy Graham's Mission England in 1986 and are based on Jesus' teaching on the importance of two or three agreeing in prayer (Matthew 18:19–20). Prayer Triplets are very simple. Three people agree to meet together regularly and each pray for three people who are not yet Christians. When these were started, over thirty thousand groups all over the UK were praying before and during the Mission, and many people responded to the challenge of Christ. Prayer Triplets are still used today, especially in connection with a specific evangelistic event or mission. Some of the Mission England Triplets have also continued; I recently met someone who has seen many come to faith in Christ over the years, as he and his two prayer partners continue to meet together regularly.

We can pray at a prayer meeting

Many churches hold special prayer meetings either on a regular basis or occasionally during the year. I recently took part in two very different but exciting occasions. One was held in the East End of London in

a black-led church. We spent the whole night in worship and prayer for issues relating to reconciliation between the different ethnic groups in our nation. I have to admit I arrived at the meeting exhausted after a week's work – but I left totally refreshed and renewed at six the next morning! The second event was held in a large church in Kensington. Six hundred people had just spent the day together learning about how to mobilise prayer in their churches, and the last hour was given to a prayer meeting. We prayed in pairs, in threes and in small groups. We prayed in silence and we prayed out loud together. At one point half of us worshipped through song and the other half prayed. With good leadership and a balance of worship, thanksgiving, confession and asking, I believe any church can put on 'a good prayer meeting'!

We can pray in a prayer group

This is very similar to a Prayer Triplet, except that the numbers are not limited to three people and the focus of the group will not just be evangelistic. Many churches have prayer groups which pray for different areas of the life of the Church, such as children, young people and missionaries. A more recent development in many English towns and cities is the start of regular inter-church prayer groups to pray for specific issues that affect a whole community. Nottingham, for example, has for a number of years had prayer groups praying not only for each area of the town but also for what they call the pillars of the community – police, education, health service, business, council and trade unions. Each prayer 'task force' links up with a Christian in each of those sectors who regularly updates them on prayer needs.

Overcoming the difficulties

In spite of the fact that praying with others can be so rewarding and exciting, many people find it difficult to join in with such groups. I think there are a number of reasons for this.

- First, as we pray on our own, we develop our ways of talking with God, and it can be a shock when we move from that intimacy with God to praying with others. We need to appreciate that we all pray differently. Some like to use written prayers, others like to pray using their own words (called extempore prayer) and others prefer to pray in silence. However, as a group of people get to know each other, it is amazing how all the different ways of praying can be blended together.
- Second, we need to recognise that some people feel daunted when praying in a larger group. We need to remind ourselves that we are not there to please ourselves but our heavenly Father. He is prompting

us by his Spirit to pray. What we have to do is to follow his leading. Others may feel that they never say the right words, or find that their prayer has just been said by someone else. If it does happen that someone prays for what you were going to pray for, be encouraged that you have been led to pray for the same thing, and pray your prayer. As you pray, others will then be able to pick up and stay with that topic until the Lord leads on to something else. If you feel tongue-tied or nervous, why not turn to your Bible or service book and pray a prayer from there, or write your own prayer to read out during the prayer meeting?

- Third, one of the most common difficulties is simply not being able to hear what others are praying. I have yet to find out why most British Christians put their heads down, rest their hands on their heads and address the floor when they start to talk to God! We need to encourage people to speak out, to keep their heads up and avoid using this 'Protestant hair shampoo' position!

- Fourth, it is easy to do too much talking and not enough praying. To help overcome this, why not try conversational praying? For example, I might pray for my neighbour John because he has just lost his job. The group is not aware of this so Bill asks me about it. I share a little more and Bill then goes on to pray.

Whatever the difficulties, we can always seek to find

opportunities to pray with others in our homes, our workplaces, down the phone or on the web. Corporate prayer is powerful, as this story from South America shows.

In the early 1990s, the situation in Cali was serious: the Columbian city was reportedly controlled by the largest, richest and most well-organised cocaine cartel in history. But a small group of Christians started to pray together. They despaired of the powerlessness of the Church, the lack of co-operation among church leaders and the appalling levels of crime and violence. After praying together for several years, four pastors decided to hire the city's stadium and spend a night in prayer and repentance in May 1995. To their amazement, twenty-six thousand people turned up to pray for the city through the night. They prayed about the crime rate. Forty-eight hours later, the daily newspaper carried the headline 'No Homicides'. For the first time as long as anyone could remember, a 24-hour period had passed when no one had been killed. Ninety days later, they held another all-night prayer meeting and sixty-five thousand people came. They prayed for the area of corruption. Within weeks, over nine hundred cartel-linked officers were fired from the police force. Since then, the Columbian Church has faced many challenges. One of the original four pastors was murdered. But the Christians in Cali have continued to pray together, and the results are staggering as they have watched their society being transformed by the mercy and grace of God.[2]

A prayer for amateurs

Our Father, thank you that you are always with us and we are never alone. Help me to find ways to pray with and for others. Amen.

10

Prayer is a mighty weapon

Prayer is not just a relationship with God: it is also a powerful weapon. Listen to a Glaswegian who has been in prison for twenty-four years: 'I believe totally in the power of prayer. I've met several men in prison, real hard guys, who have suddenly become Christians as they have sat alone in their cell. As I talk to them about it, I always discover that a Christian – a mother, an auntie, a friend – has been praying for them over the years. I believe that I was converted by my mother's prayers. Prayer – that's got to be the answer.'

We need the weapon of prayer because there is a battle going on, between the kingdom of light and the kingdom of darkness. We have a powerful enemy, called Satan or the devil, who was thrown out of heaven for disobeying God (Revelation 12:7–9). Jesus Christ defeated the devil and all his works on the cross (Colossians 2:15). Although he is a beaten foe, with his powers limited by God, the devil is alive and at work in our world today. We need to be aware that his main aim is to make war against Christians and prevent us from following God.

However, not everyone is convinced of this today! It is interesting to note that Christians in Europe and North America find great difficulty in believing in the reality of evil, whereas Christians in the Third World (where the Church is growing the fastest) fully appreciate the battle that is raging.

Prayer is the God-given means by which God's power is brought to our defence, so we are able to stand up against the devil's schemes for ourselves and for others. For prayer makes Satan tremble. 'The one concern of the devil is to keep us the saints from praying. He fears nothing from prayerless studies, prayerless work, prayerless religion. He laughs at our toil, he mocks at our wisdom, but he trembles when we pray' (Samuel Chadwick, church leader, 1860–1932).

As Christians, we need to realise that we are completely hidden and are safe in Christ (Colossians 3:3). Jesus has provided us with all we need to stand firm. St Paul describes this in terms of a suit of armour, probably prompted by the soldiers who would have stood guard over him when he was in prison.

Stand firm then, with the belt of truth buckled around your waist, with the breastplate of righteousness in place, and with your feet fitted with the readiness that comes from the gospel of peace. In addition to all this, take up the shield of faith, with which you can extinguish all the flaming arrows of the evil one. Take the helmet of salvation and the sword of the Spirit, which is the word of God. And pray in the Spirit on all occasions with all kinds of prayers and requests. (Ephesians 6:14–18)

We are told in the letter to the Romans, 'clothe yourselves with the Lord Jesus Christ'. His life represents the armour, so we need to put on truth, righteousness, peace, faith and salvation as provided by Jesus. As a young Christian, I was given some advice which I have always found helpful. This was to imagine putting on the armour each morning as I got dressed, committing myself to the Lord for the day ahead.

Prayer and fasting

Fasting is also important. The practice of fasting occurs many times in the Bible in both the Old and New Testaments. Jesus taught about fasting and assumed that his followers would fast (Matthew 6:16–18). Paul fasted after his encounter with Jesus. The early Church also practised fasting. Many church leaders down the years have believed in its importance. For example, John Wesley (who founded the Methodist Movement) personally fasted every Wednesday and Friday. He gave much credit for the fruit and power of his ministry to the discipline of fasting. Richard Foster writes in *Celebration of*

Discipline[3] that 'the central idea in fasting is the voluntary denial of an otherwise normal function for the sake of intense spiritual activity'. We can fast from food, from people, from the media, from the phone, from the computer and from our consumer culture in order to spend time with God in prayer. Fasting enables us to humble ourselves before God, to overcome temptation, to gain understanding when seeking God's direction and to obtain God's support in order to accomplish his will. Prayer and fasting are very powerful weapons, as I have proved time and time again in praying for myself and for others.

A weapon for protection

We are told in the Lord's Prayer to pray 'lead us not into temptation'. Not only do we have our own sin to contend with, but we have the world tempting us and the devil wanting us to abandon prayer and following God altogether. We need to take our stand and to pray for God's protection for ourselves and our loved ones. The Celtic Church, which was around in Britain in the fourth and fifth centuries, was very much aware of the power of evil and had special prayers of protection, called encircling prayers and 'breastplate' prayers, in which they stated their faith in the God who was able to protect them. The most famous of these is called 'St Patrick's Breastplate' and is a favourite hymn in many churches today.

We can be prompted to pray for protection in the most surprising of ways. A friend and I arrived in Bradford, the evening before we were due to go to the Maundy Service in the cathedral to be attended by the Queen and Prince Philip. Our hotel had provided a kettle in the bedroom, and we immediately put it on for a welcome cup of tea. It did not work; eventually we had to take it to the manager, who told us the fuse was faulty. Later on that evening, I had to go out. When I returned, my friend told me of how the Lord had reminded her of the fuse on the kettle and she had found herself praying for protection for the cathedral. A few days later, we found out that at the exact time she was praying, a device with fuses had been discovered in the cathedral, and safely disposed of!

A weapon in evangelism

Jesus has given us authority to go and make disciples of all nations and spread the news of his kingdom (Matthew 28:18–20). Prayer enables us to take action against the kingdom of darkness as it impinges on our lives and on the lives of others (2 Corinthians 10:3–5). A church in America decided to test whether it made any difference if they prayed before they contacted people who lived nearby. They selected an area of 160 houses and divided them into two blocks: eighty were prayed for by the congregation and eighty were not. After a few months, the church secretary rang all 160 homes. She told them who she was and asked if they had any prayer requests for the church to pray about, or whether they would like a visit from someone in the church. When she called the eighty homes that had not been prayed for, one person responded with a prayer request. When she called the other block, which had been prayed for, she found that sixty-seven people responded with prayer requests and more than forty asked for visits from the church. Prayer had opened the door for them to begin to hear.

A weapon in human battle

When the Gulf War erupted in January 1991, many Christians were called to pray and intercede. Among them were a group of intercessors in America led by Sister Gwen and her husband Lieutenant Colonel James Shaw. The night before the bombing began the Lord began to reveal to them how to pray, and they kept a record. They were first shown that if the ground troops came directly north from Saudi Arabia they would be killed by the thousands. The troops needed to make a wide arc and come into Kuwait from the west, so the group prayed that God would guide those in leadership – and General Schwarzkopf led the troops from the west. As the war went on, they were led to pray for great confusion to befall the enemy, their counsellors and their allies. This indeed happened. Next, they prayed for God to neutralise the biological and germ warfare which Hussein had threatened to use. Inexplicably, the wind turned from its normal pattern to blow back towards Iraq. They interceded for the Jewish people. Miraculously, no Jews died directly because of the Scud missile attacks.

We do well to meditate on these words of Karl Barth, a Swiss theologian, who said, 'To clasp hands in prayer is the beginning of an uprising against the disorder of the world.'

A prayer for amateurs

Mighty God, thank you for providing all I need to withstand the battle. Help me to stand firm and trust you for your help and victory. Amen.

11

Prayer – when, where, how?

When should I pray?

We can pray at any time. While we should take moments to tune in to God throughout the day, it is best to make some special time each day to meet with him. Someone has wisely noted that 'the difference between catching a few moments with the Lord or having quality time with him is like the difference between driving through McDonald's or spending the evening at a good restaurant. At the takeaway you drive up, shout your order, drive to the window and eat as you drive. In the restaurant, you sit down, spend time in fellowship, enjoy every bit and leave satisfied and nourished.' If we don't have a regular time to enjoy the company of God, we are the ones who miss out! Jesus found that his best time to talk with his Father was early in the morning (Mark 1:35).

PRAYERS

Our challenge is to find out when our best time is and then to make room for God in our busy lifestyles.

Where can I pray?

Jesus talked about the need for us to find a special place (Matthew 6:6). But we can pray anywhere – in our homes, when we travel, walking down the road or waiting in the supermarket queue. We can pray at our workplace, in the kitchen or on the golf course. A seventeenth-century monk, Brother Lawrence, developed his own way of 'practising the presence of God'. As he worked in the monastery kitchen, he learned to experience the reality of God's presence by getting into the habit of turning his heart and mind towards God throughout the day.

How long do I pray for?

This really is up to you. You may have three minutes, five minutes, fifteen minutes or an hour. The important thing is to begin with what you know you can manage. You could use the ACTS model (Adoration, Confession, Thanksgiving and Supplication) and spend a few moments on each for yourself and others and see how the Lord leads you. Or taking the framework of the Lord's Prayer use each phrase as a prompt to pray for yourself and others. I find it

helpful to divide up my prayer time and tune in to God at various points through the day. In that way I find that I can cover most of what I want to pray for. God isn't looking for long prayers, but he is looking for a heart turned towards him. Sometimes just a word or two is all we have time for or need to say. I know my most used 'arrow' prayer is 'Help, Lord!' (see Nehemiah 2:4–5).

How do I handle distractions?

All of us face this problem. As soon as we start to pray our minds are filled with everything else but him! We can helpfully do a number of things:

- if it is a matter of being reminded of all that needs to be done, keep a pencil and paper handy and write a list;
- if we are bombarded with thoughts or images that are obviously not from God, we need to ask God to remove them from our mind;
- if we are suddenly reminded of a person or situation that concerns us, then pray;
- if the phone keeps ringing, either ignore it, unplug it or use an answerphone;
- I find it good to read a passage of scripture aloud to focus my thoughts again.

How can I remember what to pray for?

There are a number of ways to keep track of our prayers. You need to choose whichever seems most appropriate for you.

- A Prayer Journal can be helpful. We can use it to record our times of prayer, write down favourite prayers of others and write our prayers to God.
- A Prayer Diary is useful for recording what we pray for others and how we receive answers. All you need is a page with columns, which give the date, name of person, prayer request and prayer answered. I vividly remember a time when a number of us in the home group in Oxford kept such a diary at our weekly early-morning prayer meeting. We were amazed when we started to keep a record of just how much God did answer prayer!
- Prayer Lists are good if you like lists! You can have a daily, weekly or monthly list in which you choose two or three people or issues for each day.
- A photoboard is excellent – especially when praying with children and for those you don't see on a regular basis.

Do I have to pray aloud?

Praying out loud is no more important than praying silently, but it helps if you want others to pray with you! If you want to start to pray out loud, write out your prayer and get used to hearing your own voice on your own. Another way is to read a verse of scripture and then pray it back to God aloud. For example, take Matthew chapter 6 verse 34: 'Therefore do not worry about tomorrow, for tomorrow will worry about itself. Each day has enough trouble of its own.' After reading this we could pray, 'Thank you, Lord, that you have promised that we do not need to worry. Please help me not to worry about . . . (list the things you are worried about) and help me trust you for today.'

Should I sit, kneel or stand?

It does not matter to God whether we stand, kneel, sit, walk or lie down prostrate on the floor. We need to do whatever feels most 'right' for us. I find I want to sit sometimes, kneel at others or go for a walk on other occasions. Most people like to start their times of prayer by 'centring down', when it is suggested that we sit comfortably on a chair, back straight, feet on the floor and begin to relax, breathing out the tensions of the day and breathing in the Lord's love and peace.

What is important is for each of us to offer our whole selves to God when we come to prayer (Romans 12:1). Here are two ways to use our hands.

- Start with clenched fists. As you praise and confess to God, you can open your hands as you receive his love and cleansing.
- Cup your hands (as if holding something in them) as you give thanks for all you have received from God in the day (or last week) in silence. Then reach out with your hands (as if to show God the needs of those on your heart, or his suffering world) and pray for those in need and in pain. Finally, lift up your hands (as if to welcome) and express your trust and hope in God.

A prayer for amateurs

Lord Jesus, I still have many questions about prayer. But what I want to do is start. Please show me when is my best time and help me to get going. Amen.

12

Prayer is not always easy

Prayer is a huge subject and we have only touched on the tip of it in this short book. We need to look at one more important area – coping with difficulties in prayer – for I would not want to give the impression that prayer is easy, or that all prayers get answered quickly. Prayer is not meant to be easy and it is not something we can just skip over and only do when the mood takes us. For prayer is one of the most important tasks that God has given to his children. It will often be hard work and a real struggle, but we need to persevere.

Most of us, if we are honest, will admit that we find prayer difficult. It demands time, which we never seem to have. It requires concentration, when our minds and thoughts are on other things. It calls for endless patience.

How do we cope? Here are some helpful tips I have learned over the years.

First, we need to make prayer part of our lives, indeed a habit, if we want to learn to pray. Experts tell us that it takes the average person thirty days doing the same thing before it becomes a habit. We need to become disciplined and make a habit of meeting with God. I know people who put in their diary a lunch-hour with God each week, or extended time at weekends when it is not possible in the week.

Second, we need to remember to 'pray as you can and not as you can't'. I meet so many people who feel guilty about what they are *not* doing when it comes to prayer that they just never get started. God certainly doesn't want us to remain this way. We need to confess our failure. But then pray as you can, for the time you can manage, asking God by his Spirit to lead and guide. And remember: just wanting to pray is prayer; a sigh is prayer; tears can be prayer; for God knows what is on our hearts.

Third, we need to understand that our time is not the same as God's time and we have to learn to wait for God. I find this very difficult. Fortunately, I have a wise friend who is always reminding me that 'God is never in a hurry, as his timing is always perfect'! I believe God does answer prayers when we really want to please him and serve others. But he does not necessarily do so in the way that we want, because he sees the bigger picture and he knows how it all fits together. Looking at the wrong side of a piece of tapestry, it is hard to imagine that there is a picture in the making. Threads are hanging waiting to be linked up again, and colours seem to run everywhere. But when you turn it over and see the right side, each thread is waiting its turn to be woven in. It is much the same with our prayers. They each have their turn to be slotted in to make the picture complete.

Fourth, we need to remember that sin is a barrier to our prayers being heard by God. He is not able to answer our prayers if we know of unconfessed sin in our hearts (Isaiah 59:2), if we are disobedient to what he may have asked us to do (1 John 3:21–2), if we have wrong motives in our asking (James 4:2–3), or if we haven't bothered to find out what his will is in a given situation.

God's answers usually come in five ways. He may answer with a 'Yes – I thought you'd never ask' reply. These replies usually come very quickly. He may answer with a 'Yes – but not yet' reply. This is much more difficult to handle. When I first became a Christian, I found that I received answers much more quickly than I do now. This is the time when we need to hold on to God and not let go, just because we can't understand.

God may answer 'Yes, but not in the way you think'. One month before the elections in South Africa in 1994, a policeman was praying about the situation when he was visited by an angel. The angel told him, 'I want South Africa on its knees in prayer. You have fourteen days to go to the highest authority . . .' The policeman was astonished, but went and did as he was told. He went to President de Klerk, who agreed, and 6 April – Founders' Day – was declared a day of prayer for South Africa. Many believe that this opened the final way for the agreement to be reached. I don't for one moment think that the policeman thought he would be involved in that way. We have to be willing to be part of the answer to our own prayers!

God may answer with a 'No, I love you too much.' These are the answers which we only discover when we look back on a situation. Sometimes we ask for things that are just not right for us. We act as if we are three-year-olds asking our parents for an electric drill for Christmas! I remember hearing Ruth Graham (wife of Billy Graham) talking about this. She recounted the story of how she prayed and prayed for the man she thought she wanted to marry. Today, she is so grateful to God that he did not answer her prayer. For at that time she had not yet met Billy, and she now realises what a disaster the other marriage would have been!

And God may answer with what appears to be a straight 'No'. This is very hard to handle, especially when you are praying for a loved one who is sick, a member of your family to find faith in Christ or someone suffering from addiction. Just this week I have heard about the death of a Sheffield church leader whom I greatly respected. Many people had been praying for his recovery, and it just had not happened. At this point we don't understand why. Fiona Castle, speaking after the death of her husband Roy, said, 'I would never underestimate the value of prayer. I really believe that although perhaps prayer was not answered in the way we would have liked to see it answered in I honestly believe that through the prayers of the faithful people who prayed for Roy . . . he was strong, he was faithful to the end. I believe that through prayer we were given opportunities to share our faith.' We need to remember that there is so much more to healing than physical healing, and to be with God in heaven, where there is no more crying and no more pain, is for many the best healing there could ever be.

Fifth, we need to learn to hold on to God's promises when he seems far away. Most of us, at some period in our Christian life, will experience a time when it feels as if God has gone on a long walk and left us far behind. It may last for a few days, weeks, months or even longer. Sometimes it is because we have unconfessed sin in our lives, but more often it is simply God teaching us to depend on him more and more. It can take many forms. You may find Bible-reading dull, your prayers may feel as if they are hitting the ceiling, or you may experience doubts about your faith. If you can, find another Christian to pray with and for you, stick with reading the Bible, and use books of prayers to keep in touch with God when your own words dry up. He will come to you in his time and in his way.

Sixth, we can find out more about prayer. We can study prayers in the Bible: for example, Moses praying for Joshua (Exodus 17:8–13); Daniel praying for his nation (Daniel 9); Hannah praying for a child (1 Samuel 1:10–16); Jesus praying for his disciples

(John 17); Paul praying for a church (Colossians 1:3–8; Ephesians 3:14–19).

We can read books about prayer: for example, Richard Foster's *Prayer*[4] is a modern classic exploring all aspects of prayer; Rob Warner's *Praying with Jesus*[5] looks at the Lord's Prayer; Jeremy Jennings' *The Church on its Knees*[6] is about dynamic prayer in the local church. Other books include: *Saints at Prayer*,[7] an excellent course for small groups; *Don't Just Stand There . . . Pray Something*,[8] which concentrates on intercession; *The Word Is Very Near You*,[9] which helps you to pray with scripture; *Praying through Life*,[10] which is a practical book and helpful if you like using written prayers; and *Community Prayer Cells: How to be Good News Neighbours*,[11] which explores the subject of prayer and evangelism.

Whatever your experience of prayer, remember to be honest with yourself and God – he can handle it! And remember: he will never leave you or forsake you (Matthew 28:20).

A prayer for amateurs

Loving Lord, yes, I have found prayer difficult and sometimes have not known how to begin. Please help me not to be put off by what I can't do. I do want to follow you, love you and trust you more. Amen.

Notes

1 Richard Foster, *Prayer* (Hodder & Stoughton, 1992).
2 The dramatic change that has taken place in Cali is described in G Otis's book *Informed Intercession* (Regal, 1999).
3 Richard Foster, *Celebration of Discipline* (Hodder & Stoughton, 1980).
4 Foster, *Prayer.*
5 Rob Warner, *Praying with Jesus* (Hodder & Stoughton, 1999).
6 Jeremy Jennings, *The Church on its Knees* (HTB, 1998).
7 *Saints at Prayer* (Lynx Communications, 1994).
8 Ronald Dunn, *Don't Just Stand There ... Pray Something* (Scripture Press, 1991).
9 Martin Smith, *The World is Very Near You* (DLT, 1990).
10 Stephen Cottrell, *Praying through Life* (Church House Publishing, 1998).
11 Jane Holloway, *Community Prayer Cells: How to be Good News Neighbours* (CPAS, 1998).

Evangelism for Amateurs

Michael Green

EVANGELISM MAKES MOST OF US FEEL TOTALLY INADEQUATE

We simply feel like running for cover: the last thing we want to be seen as is mindless enthusiasts pushing our views on other people. But if we are to follow Jesus' command to go and make disciples, it isn't something we can just ignore.

Evangelism for Amateurs is full of ideas on reaching out to our families, friends and neighbours in a way that is relaxed, 'human', and possible even to those of us who feel unqualified for the job.

There are guidelines for talking to those who feel that 'my view is as good as yours', or for whom churchgoing is something they wouldn't normally even consider, making this book highly relevant to today's cultural climate.

Rather than 'highjacking' people with the gospel, we can confidently begin to help them find a living faith for themselves.

Hodder & Stoughton
0 340 71420 4

Holy Communion for Amateurs

Tom Wright

Most Christians obey Jesus' command to 'Do this in remembrance of me': breaking bread and drinking wine as he did at the Last Supper.

BUT MANY OF US HAVE ONLY A LITTLE UNDERSTANDING OF WHY WE DO THIS, AND WHAT IT MEANS.

Theories and beliefs about this central Christian practice have, sadly, often divided Christians. Without clear teaching all sorts of misunderstandings creep in, and Christians fail to benefit from this wonderful and central action of faith.

This book explains in a clear and lively fashion the background to the Last Supper, the ways in which Christians have interpreted Jesus' actions over the centuries, and what it all means for us today.

It will be valued by all who want to understand what they are doing in coming to the Lord's table. It will serve as an excellent introduction to the topic at a Confirmation class, or for anyone wanting a refresher course on this aspect of basic Christianity.

Hodder & Stoughton
0 340 74579 7

Theology for Amateurs

Alister McGrath

MANY OF US FIND THEOLOGY DIFFICULT OR IRRELEVANT

Written clearly and simply by one of the world's best-known and respected theologians, this book shows how theology can actually add new depth to our faith.

Many Christians have only scratched the surface of the gospel. *Theology for Amateurs* shows us how to go deeper. Theology can strengthen our personal faith, stimulate our minds and enrich our worship. Theology brings our minds and hearts together, and sets them on fire with wonder and amazement.

Yet theology is not only exciting. It is useful! One of Alister McGrath's main themes is that good theology leads on to good apologetics and evangelism. The more we understand the gospel, the more effectively we can explain and proclaim it.

Ideal for personal and group study, this important book will be welcomed by all who want to understand the Christian faith for all its worth.

Hodder & Stoughton
0 340 74553 3